PRAYERS ON THE
PSALMS

PRAYERS ON THE
PSALMS

From the

SCOTTISH PSALTER
1595

With an Introduction by
David B. Calhoun

THE BANNER OF TRUTH TRUST

THE BANNER OF TRUTH TRUST
3 Murrayfield Road, Edinburgh EH12 6EL, UK
P.O. Box 621, Carlisle, PA 17013, USA

*

© Banner of Truth Trust 2010

ISBN-13: 978 1 84871 095 5

*

Typeset in 10.5 / 13.5 pt Adobe Caslon Pro
at the Banner of Truth Trust, Edinburgh

Printed in the USA by
Versa Press, Inc.,
East Peoria, IL

INTRODUCTION

Books for Scottish Presbyterian worship services go back to the days of John Knox. *The Forme of Prayers and Ministration of the Sacraments* was prepared by Knox in Frankfurt and published in Geneva in 1556. Encouraged by Calvin and the example of the French Psalter, Knox and the Protestant refugees in Geneva also published their own Anglo-Genevan Psalter, with eighty-seven Psalms and many French tunes. In 1564 the complete psalter, known as the St Andrews Psalter, was issued as part of the Book of Common Order.[1]

[1] So emerged the 'Old Scottish Psalter', which lasted

A later edition of the Scottish Psalter, published in 1595, was titled *The Psalms of David in Metre, According as they are sung in the Kirk of Scotland, Together with the Conclusion, or Gloria Patri, after the Psalme: and also one Prayer after every Psalme, agreing with the meaning therof.* Charles Greig M'Crie believes this psalter was 'epoch-marking in the history of Scottish Presbyterian worship'.[1]

---

until 1650. Thomas Young writes: 'The Old Scottish Psalter, as the years rolled on, became dear, and ever more dear, to the Scottish people . . . It had become familiar to them through their use of it in private and public worship. It linked them to Geneva — the cradle of their Calvinistic theology, and the refuge of their banished fellow-countrymen. Their martyrs had sung its consoling strains in dungeons, in exile, and in their dying hours' (Thomas Young, quoted in *The Scottish Metrical Psalter: Its Story and Influence*, p. 7.)

[1] M'Crie, *The Public Worship of Presbyterian Scotland*, p. 136.

The Psalter of 1595 contained several exceptional features. First, there are thirty-five metrical doxologies, called 'Conclusions', one adapted to each form of metre used in the Psalter.[1] Second, the metrical and prose portions of this psalter were published separately. The preface stated that the second book was for 'the ease of men in travel, and being from their home, who gladly would carry a thin book

---

[1] The doxologies are given in full and exactly as printed in M'Crie, *The Public Worship of Presbyterian Scotland*, Appendix 1, pp. 386–9. For Psalm 25, for example, the text of the doxology is as follows:

> O Lord the strength and rock,
>   of all that traist in thee:
> Saif and defend thy chosen flock
>   from all calamitie.
> Gloir to the Father be
>   the Sonne and halie Gaist:
> As it hes bene continuallie,
>   is now, and euer shall last.

(as this of the prayers is) that cannot easily carry the whole Psalms.' Besides that, poor children who could not buy the whole psalter could purchase the little book (which included the Catechism) for an 'easy price'. Thirdly, the 1595 Psalter was unique in including short prayers, one for each Psalm, summarizing the content of that Psalm. Millar Patrick claims that 'the prayers given with the Psalms, one for each, are in the finest Scottish diction of the period.'[1]

What is the origin or source for these 'Prayers on the Psalms'?

In the English Psalter, usually known as that of Archbishop Parker, who died in 1575, there is a 'collecte' added after each Psalm. Neil Livingstone believed that this was 'the only known precedent' for the prayers

---

[1] Patrick, *Four Centuries of Scottish Psalmody*, p. 53.

of the 1595 Scottish book. David Douglas Bannerman speculates that Parker's prayers may have suggested the Scottish 'Prayers on the Psalms', but he judges that the Scottish prayers are 'decidedly superior in simplicity, fervour and power of expression'.[1]

The famous Edinburgh printer Thomas Bassandyne listed in his will or inventory of 1578 a book with the title *Prayers upon the Psalms*. These may be the collects of 1595 printed separately before they were included in the authorized Psalter, but it seems more likely that it is a publication of the English prayers of Parker.

The 'Prayers on the Psalms' were long supposed to be of genuine Scottish origin, although a number of French words used in the Scottish prayers might suggest a French

[1] Bannerman, *The Worship of the Presbyterian Church*, p. 92.

source.[1] The relations between Scotland and France at that time, however, were so close that extensive borrowing from the French language could be explained on historical rather than literary grounds.

In 1885, David Douglas Bannerman, minister of the Free Church in Dalkeith, came upon a copy of a French Psalter of Marot and Beza among the books of the old Innerpeffray Library. The title of the little volume ended with the words 'and a Prayer at the end of each Psalm by M. Augustin Marlorat'. This book was published in Paris in 1567. Bannerman was convinced that the Scottish 'Prayers on the Psalms' were, for all practical purposes, translations of the

---

[1] M'Crie writes that Livingston was inclined to regard the 'Prayers on the Psalms' as 'of purely Scottish extraction'. M'Crie, *The Public Worship of Presbyterian Scotland*, p. 139.

French *'Oraisons'* of Marlorat. The Scottish prayers were 'sentence for sentence and word for word' translations of the French prayers.[1] M. Bovet, historian of the *Psalter of the Reformed Churches*, stated that 'Marlorat was the original and the only author of the prayers which bear his name.' The connection between the Scottish prayers and those of Marlorat furnished 'fresh evidence of the close and cordial relations which subsisted from the first between the Reformed Churches of the Continent and the Church of Scotland'.[2]

Augustin Marlorat was an honoured colleague of Calvin and Beza in the Genevan Reformation.[3] He was born

[1] Bannerman, *Presbyterian Review* 7 (1886), p. 155, quoted by Patrick, *The Scottish Collects*, p. 4.
[2] M'Crie, *The Public Worship of Presbyterian Scotland*, p. 139.
[3] This summary of Marlorat's life is based on the

in Lorraine in 1506. When he was eight years old, he was placed in an Augustinian monastery and took the name of the great patron of his order. He was ordained as a priest aged eighteen and, in 1533, became abbot of a monastery in Bourges. He began to be influenced by Protestant teaching, however, and was forced to flee from France in 1535. He went to Geneva, where he gained a precarious living as a proof-reader for Greek and Hebrew texts. At the recommendation of Pierre Viret,

---

entry in *The New Schaff-Herzog Encyclopedia of Religious Knowledge*, VII, p. 186; and Henry Martyn Baird, *Theodore Beza: The Counsellor of the French Reformation, 1519–1605*, p. 156. M'Crie describes Marlorat as 'an honoured theologian, devotional writer, and reformer of the sixteenth century, the friend of Calvin, the coadjutor of Beza, and ultimately a victim of Roman Catholic intolerance and cruelty at the siege and capture of Rouen in 1562' (*The Public Worship of Presbyterian Scotland*, p. 139).

Augustin Marlorat was appointed pastor in Crassier near Lausanne, and he married during his time there. From Crassier he was called to Vevey, where he served until 1559.

After another brief sojourn in Geneva, Marlorat was sent to Paris to be pastor of the Protestant congregation in the city. In 1560 he became the first Protestant preacher in Rouen, a city where Protestants were struggling to secure the right to hold public services. On the accession of Charles IX in December 1560, the Protestants addressed a petition, written by Marlorat, to the parliament and king, requesting permission for the use of a building for worship. Their request was refused, but the ten thousand Protestants of Rouen defied the edict and held services in the halls of the town's ancient tower. Marlorat sent a petition to

Catherine de' Medici, in which he asserted the loyalty of Protestants to the state. In August 1561 he was one of the Protestant leaders, with Theodore Beza, who took part in the disputation with Catholics at Poissy, and was also present at the disputation before the leaders of the Sorbonne in January 1562.

Returning to Rouen, Marlorat presided over a synod of Huguenot churches. Civil war erupted in France at that time and, following the massacre of many Protestants elsewhere in the country, the Protestants of Rouen seized the city on April 15, 1562. Marlorat was appointed one of the three leading figures in the new government, which still professed loyalty to the king. The city held out for some months, until late September. Marlorat and the other

Protestant leaders would accept no terms that did not include the free exercise of the Protestant religion. On October 26 the city fell, and Marlorat and his family were captured and imprisoned. Three days later he was tried for treason and, on October 30, was condemned. The sentence of execution was carried out the following day. His wife and children escaped to England.

Marlorat wrote many books, marked by erudition and clarity, including commentaries on Genesis, the Psalms, the Song of Solomon, Isaiah, Mark, Luke, John, and Revelation. His New Testament commentaries were translated into English during the sixteenth century. He also produced a valuable and much used index to Calvin's *Institutes*. In their writings the Puritan divines often refer to 'Marloratus' as a competent authority on Bible and theology.[1]

'In the long list of honoured ministers of the Gospel of Christ in France who sealed their testimony with their blood, few names called forth, not in France only, but in reformed Christendom, a warmer feeling of love and reverence than that which gathered round the name Augustin Marlorat.'[2]

Marlorat's prayers first appeared in the French Psalter in 1563, the year after his death. His prayers were used in the successive editions of the French Psalter until at least 1674.

[1] C. H. Spurgeon also commends his exposition of Matthew as containing 'the cream of the earlier writers' in *Commenting and Commentaries* (see *Lectures to My Students*, repr. Edinburgh: Banner of Truth, 2008, p. 854).
[2] Patrick, *The Scottish Collects*, p. 5. The source of the quotation is not given.

The unknown translator of Marlorat's prayers for the Scottish Metrical Psalter of 1595 follows the French text carefully but 'uses a wise freedom . . . to increase the emphasis, or obviate ambiguity, or bring out the meaning of a phrase, or secure the musical flow of the rhythm.'[1]

Why were the prayers not included in any later edition of the Scottish Psalter? Millar Patrick writes that 'at so early a period the reason could not have been antipathy to the reading of printed prayers, for the Book of Common Order of 1564, which included prayers, was in general use.'[2] The appearance of the prayers in the Psalter of the Church seems to point to use in public worship, but they were printed

---

[1] Patrick, *The Scottish Collects*, p. 7.
[2] Ibid., p. 3.

in only one edition of the Psalter, and there is no reference to them in later versions. M'Crie judges that the prayers were intended not for public but for 'private use, guidance, and edification'.[1]

These little 'Prayers on the Psalms' have all but disappeared from Scottish Presbyterian worship and even from its history.[2] Annie Small comments that the prayers

---

[1] M'Crie, *The Public Worship of Presbyterian Scotland*, p. 138.
[2] Alexander Henderson possibly referred to these prayers half a century after their publication. He had been asked by the General Assembly to draft a new form of service in which the churches of England and Scotland might agree. 'With his usual wisdom', as Bannerman puts it, he declined for two reasons: the Scottish Church 'ought to carefully avoid even the appearance of dictating to the English'; and he could not take it upon himself to set down other forms of prayer than those that we have in our Psalm-book, 'penned by our great and divine Reformers' (Bannerman, *The Worship of the Presbyterian Church*, pp. 65, 66).

'are a part of our Scottish heritage which we have practically forgotten'.[1] Bannerman states that 'few people are aware . . . that in the last decade of the sixteenth century, when the Church of Scotland was in the very flower of its Presbyterianism, and the star of Andrew Melville rode highest, there were in use here by Church authority no fewer than one hundred and forty-nine collects' (one prayer was used for two psalms).[2]

The prayers are collects consisting of five parts: an invocation; some doctrine or fact of the Bible that is made the basis of the petition; the petition itself; a statement of what answer is to be expected; and a conclusion that is a pleading of the name

[1] Small, *Ancient Scottish Prayers*, p. 11.
[2] Bannerman, *The Worship of the Presbyterian Church*, p. 64.

of the Lord as the ground of confidence that the prayer will be accepted. In the last ten prayers the translator, for some reason, as his task neared its end, abandoned the collect form altogether, so that these closing prayers have little connection with the French text. The collect was quite unusual in Scottish use, but was commonly employed by Cranmer and others in England. They translated ancient Latin collects and created new prayers after the same model, whereas the Scots preferred to frame their prayers 'on a larger and looser scale'.[1]

In the 'Prayers on the Psalms' for this new edition, I have reproduced the text that appears in Appendix K in M'Crie's, *The Public Worship of Presbyterian Scotland*. Only minor changes have been made, such

[1] Patrick, *The Scottish Collects*, p. 6.

as the use of 'hope' for 'esperance', 'powers' for 'puissances', 'spoiled' for 'spulzeit', etc. Thanks to the Covenant Seminary Library, and especially to Denise Pakala for great perseverance in tracking down and obtaining Millar Patrick's *Scottish Collects from the Scottish Metrical Psalter of 1595*.

BIBLIOGRAPHY

BANNERMAN, David Douglas, *The Worship of the Presbyterian Church, with Special Reference to the Question of Liturgies*, (Edinburgh: Andrew Elliot, 1884).

Bannerman includes a selection of fifty-one of the collects with modern spelling and punctuation, but retaining most of the original words. He 'reluctantly translated' a number of purely Scottish words, 'although the nearest English equivalent is often a very inadequate substitute'. Thus, 'looking for' or 'awaiting' in the place of 'the fine Scots word', *abidand*; 'frailty' for *bruckilness*; and 'overthrow' for *dounthring*.

He groups the prayers according to their subject matter under the headings: (1) Prayers relating to individual Christian life and experience; (2) Prayers for blessing in the use of the means of grace; (3) Prayers for the Church; (4) Prayers for the nation and its rulers; (5) Prayers bearing on a Christian's relation to others; and (6) Thanksgiving and praise to God.

——, 'Origin of the Scottish Collects of 1595: A Discovery', *Presbyterian Review*, vol. 7 (1886), pp. 151–5.

LIVINGSTON, Neil, *The Scottish Metrical Psalter of A.D. 1635*, (Glasgow: Maclure and Macdonald, 1864).

In this book, the Free Church minister of Stair (Ayrshire) provides the full text of the original prayers of 1595 in an appendix, pp. ix–xviii.

M‘CRIE, Charles Greig, *The Public Worship of Presbyterian Scotland Historically Treated,* (Edinburgh and London: William Blackwood and Sons, 1892).

M‘Crie reproduces the Scottish Collects in an appendix, pp. 390–421. He was, he wrote, 'not without hope these Scottish prayers may prove of suggestive value to ministers in their conduct of Divine Service'. While adhering closely to the original prayers, he alters to some extent the 'archaic sixteenth-century form'. He does not organize the prayers under headings, 'preferring to give each collect in connection with the psalm upon which it is founded, there being often a striking connection between the former and the latter'.

PATRICK, Millar, *Four Centuries of Scottish Psalmody,* (London: Oxford University Press, 1949).

——, *The Scottish Collects from the Scottish Metrical Psalter of 1595,* (Edinburgh: Church of Scotland Committee on Publications, n. d.).

Patrick provides the best introduction to the Collects, and the most recent translation of them.

SMALL, Annie H., *Ancient Scottish Prayers with introduction by Annie H. Small,* (London & Edinburgh: T. N. Foulis, 1912).

Small gives fifty-seven of the prayers in their original form, but arranges them according to the topics: (1) For deliverance from the thraldom of sin; (2) For a holy life; (3) Thankfulness and praise; (4) For brotherly charity; (5) For the people; (6) For the kirk; (7) For the crowne and kingdom of Jesus Christ; and (8) For the whole world.

She comments that Scotland's 'religious history is not yet closed: she has duty within herself, which she owes to herself and to her 'chief end', which, when fulfilled, may send her forth upon a mission beyond herself far greater than she has ever dreamt.'

She hopes for the reviving of Scotland's 'ancient church', adding that this will be furthered by 'the sympathetic study of Scottish religious history'.

NOTE ON THE
IMPRECATORY PSALMS

We are at first surprised at the frequency with which the 'Prayers on the Psalms' call for deliverance from and the punishment of the church's enemies. A quick review of the Psalms, however, reminds us that the Psalms themselves are indeed filled with cries of anger and urgent, sometimes strident, demands that God do something about these enemies. In Psalm 25, to take just one example, David pleads with God, 'Let me not be put to shame; let not my enemies exult over me' (verse 2). He wants God to 'consider how many' are his foes and 'with what violent hatred' they hate him (verse 19).

The French author and the Scottish translator of these prayers frequently included cries to God to deliver his people from their foes and to punish those enemies so that all people would know that God cares for his own. This is not surprising when we realize that Marlorat was a French Huguenot who was executed for his Protestant convictions. The whole history of the Huguenots is marked by long-lasting persecution and suffering – and they found great support in the Psalms, especially in Psalms of judgment and deliverance, such as Psalms 46, 68, 76, and 124.

James Hastings Nichols writes:

For every occasion, it seems, an appropriate verse would leap to the tongue of a Huguenot. And all over France, wherever Huguenots of the first generation were confined, often sometimes by the score, guards and jailers became familiar with the psalms, even to prisons on Santo Domingo and Martinique . . . The courage and joy of these martyrs who, like ancient Christians, could have had release for a word, won converts among the onlookers. The authorities tried gags, but the cord would burn and from out of the smoke the psalm would again begin. The bishops then ordered that the tongues of the Huguenots should be cut out before they were burned.[1]

Scottish Presbyterianism was flourishing when the Psalter of 1595 was published,[2]

[1] James Hastings Nichols, *Corporate Worship in the Reformed Tradition*, (Philadelphia: The Westminster Press, 1968), pp. 38, 39.
[2] [Though, as Iain Murray has reminded us, the 1590s were already 'dark days' for faithful individuals like Robert Bruce (c. 1555–1631). See 'Robert Bruce: Standing Fast in Dark Days', in *A Scottish Christian Heritage* (Edinburgh: Banner of Truth, 2006, pp. 37–72). (Ed.)]

but soon it found itself in an increasingly precarious situation. The Stuart king, James VI (James I of England), pressed the church more and more to conform to his wishes. The Presbyterians resisted with patience until 1638, when the National Covenant united many in more active opposition to the attempts of King Charles I and Archbishop Laud to force the Scots to accept an episcopal form of church government and worship. After the Restoration of 1660 the Scottish Presbyterian cause became desperate as the Covenanters resisted unto death the attempt to force them to abandon their Presbyterianism. The Psalms became the heart cries of many Scots during the dark years of persecution and the 'killing time', when Covenanters were imprisoned, exiled, or killed.

In his story, 'The Tale of Tod Lapraik', Robert Lewis Stevenson writes about Covenanters imprisoned on the Bass Rock in the cold North Sea:

There were nights of it when he [Tam Dale] was here on sentry, the place a' wheest [quiet], the frost o' winter maybe riving [splitting] the wa's, and he would hear ane o' the prisoners strike up a psalm, and the rest join in, and the blessed sounds rising from the different chalmers [chambers] – or dungeons, I would rather say – so that this auld craig [rock] in the sea was like a pairt of Heev'n.[1]

The Psalms, wrote John Calvin, are

an anatomy of all the parts of the soul; for there is not an emotion of which any one can be conscious that is not here represented as in a mirror.

[1] Robert Louis Stevenson, *The Scottish Stories and Essays* (Edinburgh: The University Press, 1989), pp. 196.

In the Psalms, the Holy Spirit has drawn to life 'all the griefs, sorrows, fears, doubts, hopes, cares, perplexities' that agitate our minds.[1] Calvin took comfort in the fact that David, 'though he had deserved well of his own people', was 'nevertheless bitterly hated by many without a cause'. This, continued Calvin, 'afforded me no small consolation when I was groundlessly assailed by the hatred of those who ought

[1] Kathleen Norris describes the harrowing experience of trying to care for her husband as he struggled against depression in a North Dakota hospital. A friend from New York phoned to offer emotional support. She asked, 'How about you? Are you seeing a doctor? Do you have something to take for this?' Kathleen answered, 'I have the psalms.' Later, in her book, she writes, about how she learned to read and love the psalms, 'all one hundred fifty.' 'Every emotion', she adds, 'is expressed, as humanity is laid bare before God and everyone.' Kathleen Norris, *Acedia & Me: A Marriage, Monks, and A Writer's Life* (New York: Riverhead Books, 2008), pp. 77, 276.

to have assisted and solaced me'.[1] With their many different expressions of how his people find their perfect answer in God, it is no wonder that the Huguenots and the Covenanters turned frequently and gratefully to the Psalms – including and especially the imprecatory Psalms – to find courage, solace, and hope in times of trouble.

In our vastly different lives (although many still know suffering and death for being Christians), how should we understand the imprecatory Psalms, and other Psalms calling for judgment and deliverance, and pray the 'Prayers on the Psalms' that are found in this book? Three helpful rules for our use of the 'imprecatory Psalms' are found in the *ESV Study Bible:* —

[1] John Calvin, *Commentary on the Book of Psalms*, tr. James Anderson (Grand Rapids: Wm. B. Eerdmans Publishing Company, 1949), pp. xxxvii, xlviii.

First, one must be clear that the people being cursed are not enemies over trivial matters; they are people who hate the faithful precisely for their faith; they mock God and use ruthless and deceitful means to suppress the godly.

Second, it is worth remembering that these curses are in poetic form and can employ extravagant and vigorous expressions. The exact fulfilment is left to God.

Third, these curses are expressions of moral indignation, not of personal vengeance. They are prayers for God to vindicate himself, displaying his righteousness for the world to see.[1]

DAVID B. CALHOUN
August 2010

---

[1] *ESV Study Bible* (Wheaton, Illinois: Crossway Bible), pp. 938.

PRAYERS ON THE PSALMS

Psalm 1

O MERCIFUL AND HEAVENLY FATHER, who hast created us unto blessedness and sovereign felicity, and hast given unto us thy holy law, to be the only rule and measure, whereby we should live well and godly, make us by thy good grace to renounce our own carnal and fleshly desires, and all evil company, eschewing the way of sinners, that we may bring forth such fruits of the Spirit that, being always under thy holy protection, we may have perfect assurance and confidence; that when thy

Son Jesus Christ, shall appear to divide the goats from the sheep, we may be accounted among the number of them that are redeemed by his blood. So be it.[1]

Psalm 2

ALMIGHTY GOD AND HEAVENLY FATHER, who hast given unto us thy dear Son to be our Lord and King, grant, we beseech thee, that thou wouldst destroy and dissipate by thy marvellous wisdom all enterprises devised and directed against him throughout the whole world; and make us so to profit and grow in his holy law and doctrine that, in all fear and reverence, we may serve thee; that in the end we may attain to that endless

---

[1] Each prayer closes with, 'So be it'. In all that follow. we have replaced this with 'AMEN'.

joy which we hope to receive through the same Jesus Christ, thy Son. AMEN.[1]

Psalm 3

O ETERNAL GOD, who, to prove and try the faith and patience of thy chosen, chastisest them with great and many tribulations, in such sort that we are unable to exist or stand up against so many assaults and enemies as lift themselves against us;

---

[1] The French original of 1567 reads: Père celeste et tout puissant, qui nous as donné et consacré ton Fils unique pour Roy et Seigneur, vueille dissiper par ta sagesse admirable toutes les entreprises qui se dressent contre luy par tout le monde, et faire que nous profitions tellement en sa saincte doctrine qu'en toute crainte et révérence nous te puissons servir, pour finalement jouir du souverain bien que nous espérons par iceluy ton Fils Jésus Christ.

grant, we beseech thee, that we may be so sure and safe under thy protection that the world may see that thou art our defence and buckler. By virtue whereof we, being victorious, may utterly despise and contemn all authorities and powers that lift themselves against thee and thy Son, Jesus Christ. AMEN.

Psalm 4

MERCIFUL LORD, fountain of all righteousness, who knowest the dangerous assaults wherewith we are assaulted on all sides, refuse not our petitions; but let us have the sure experience of thy favour, and goodness; to the intent that, what affliction soever fall upon us, we may live in peace and quietness of spirit, awaiting the eternal rest which thou hast promised to thy children, through thy dear Son, Christ Jesus our Lord. AMEN.

Psalm 5

O GOOD GOD, our King and Creator, seeing we have our whole trust in thee, and do worship thee in spirit and truth, despise not, we pray thee, the sighs and prayers of thy poor servants, oppressed and afflicted by thy enemies; and keep us continually under thy protection, until we be glorified with our Head and Saviour, Jesus Christ thy Son. AMEN.

Psalm 6

GOOD LORD, who art a just Judge, and who as a Father chastisest thy children, to drive them to unfeigned repentance, grant unto us of thy infinite goodness that the afflictions which we justly suffer for our offences may serve unto the amendment of our lives; and that in the midst of them we may have a perfect feeling of thy fatherly mercy; to the intent that, our enemies being confounded, we may praise thee with thanksgiving all the days of our life, through Jesus Christ thy Son. AMEN.

Psalm 7

O GOOD GOD, the only searcher of men's hearts, who preservest us that put our confidence in thee from danger of our enemies, lift up thy mighty arm, and put back all those that persecute us; and gather together thy church dispersed by the tyranny of godless tyrants; and keep us continually under thy mighty defence, through Jesus Christ our Lord. AMEN.

Psalm 8

ETERNAL GOD, who by thy mighty providence dost govern all creatures, we humbly beseech thee that it would please thee to visit us by thy Son, Jesus Christ, and restore us to that honour from which we were cast down by the sin of our forefathers; and that we may, in remembrance of thy great benefits toward us, celebrate thy miraculous power, both now and evermore. AMEN.

Psalm 9

ALMIGHTY GOD, who dost never despise those that trust in thee, hear the complaint of us thy poor servants and suffer not the wicked to execute their cruel enterprises against us, but take them in their own snares, to the intent that we may magnify thy holy name, through Jesus Christ. AMEN.

Psalm 10

LORD GOD, who can put in order things confused and out of order, arise and stretch forth thine arm to cast down the pride of such as lift up themselves against thee, and persecute thy little flock; to the intent that, all resistance trodden down, thou mayest be acknowledged the Saviour and Protector of all them that trust in thee, through Jesus Christ our Lord. AMEN.

Psalm 11

O LORD, who art the strength and stay of us thy poor flock, although the wicked world goes about to snare us; and [seeing] that there is no way for us to escape, but only by thy grace; grant that we may continue in thy fear and truth, [and] that we be not involved in that vengeance and punishment which thou wilt pour forth upon the wicked, when thou shalt send that great Judge, Christ Jesus thy Son, to judge the whole world. AMEN.

Psalm 12

MERCIFUL FATHER, who dost abhor all hypocrisy and lies: lift up thyself and show forth thy strength for the deliverance of thy poor servants, oppressed by the calumnies of flatterers; and strengthen us from day to day in the sure hope of thy promises, until we attain to the full fruition of the same, by the merits of Jesus Christ thy Son. AMEN.

Psalm 13

O ETERNAL GOD, and most merciful Father, who quickenost things that be dead, of thine infinite goodness give unto us quietness of heart, to the intent that we, not being overthrown with the heavy burdens of afflictions that lie upon us, may in our consciences rejoice always in thy salvation; and grant, we beseech thee, that we may continually addict ourselves to praise and magnify thy most holy name, through Jesus Christ, thy dear Son, our Redeemer. AMEN.

Psalm 14

O GOD ONLY JUST AND RIGHTEOUS, we beseech thee that it will please thee to draw us out of this fearful corruption wherewith the whole race of mankind is infected, and deliver us from the thraldom of sin, that we, walking in all simplicity and godliness, may in the end enjoy the fruit of that happy deliverance which thou hast given us by the oblation of the sacrifice of thy Son, Christ Jesus. AMEN.

Psalm 15

HEAVENLY FATHER, who hast adopted us to be thy children, grant that we, passing through this corrupt world in such integrity and cleanness that none have any just occasion to complain of us, may in the end be participant of that celestial heritage which is prepared for us in the heavens, through Jesus Christ, our only Saviour. AMEN.

Psalm 16

O LORD, who art our good God and Lawgiver, since it hath pleased thee to call us to the fellowship of those whom thou hast ordained to salvation, give us hearts that we may earnestly detest the company of infidels and idolaters, and that we may employ ourselves in magnifying thy holy name; that, living under thy defence, we may be always more and more assured of a happy life, which thou wilt give to all thine, through Jesus Christ thy Son. AMEN.

Psalm 17

O GOOD LORD, the only searcher of men's hearts, howsoever we are compassed about on all sides with infinite dangers, yet we beseech thee to show forth to us thy favour and thy good will, without which we should immediately perish. Suffer not, O Lord, that our hearts be bent on things earthly, but that we may follow thy commandments, and ever aspire to that heavenly bliss which Jesus Christ, thy Son, has acquired for us by his own blood. AMEN.

Psalm 18

O LORD, the buckler and defence of all those who love thee, hear thy poor servants who call upon thee in truth and verity, and deliver them from their enemies. And forasmuch as there is nothing better than to acknowledge and follow thy holy will, chase from us all darkness of error and ignorance; and let thy light so shine over us thy poor church that, being strengthened by thy strength, we may employ ourselves wholly in setting forth thy praises, through Jesus Christ thy dear Son. AMEN.

Psalm 19

O GOD, Creator of all things, grant that we may acknowledge and magnify thy great strength and power that declare thee in the conserving and guiding of this world. Suffer not that we wander any whit from thy holy law, which is pure and perfect, but that, taking delight therein, we may wholly be so governed by it that in the end we may be participant of the heavenly salvation, through Jesus Christ. AMEN.

Psalm 20

O EVERLASTING GOD, who art ruler and guide of all things, who hast commanded us to obey our superiors and magistrates, let it please thee, for thy mercies' sake, to extend thy mercy and blessing upon our King and Prince, and all our superiors, that they, living in thy fear and protection, may overthrow their enemies; and we, living in quietness under them, may praise thee all our lives, through Jesus Christ our Lord. AMEN.

Psalm 21

ETERNAL GOD, the only author of all good things, since it hath pleased thee to receive us into the communion of thy well-beloved Son, our Lord Jesus Christ, suffer us not in any wise to be overcome of our enemies. But grant that, his kingdom being established in the midst of us, we may triumphantly sing and magnify his praises, both now and evermore. AMEN.

Psalm 22

Although, O GOD OF ALL CONSOLATION AND COMFORT, thou sufferest us for a little season to be afflicted diverse ways, and makest us (as it were) to be the outcasts of the world, yet, forasmuch as we have our only trust in thy goodness, we beseech thee to assist us and deliver us from all those troubles that distress us, that, in the midst of thy holy congregation, we may render thee hearty praises and thanks, through Jesus Christ thy only Son. AMEN.

Psalm 23

ETERNAL AND EVERLASTING FATHER, fountain of all felicity, we render thee praise and thanks that thou hast made known to us our Pastor and Defender who will deliver us from the power of our adversaries. Grant unto us that we, casting away all fear and terror of death, may embrace and confess thy truth, which it has pleased thee to reveal to us by thy Son, our Lord and sovereign Master, Christ Jesus. Amen.

Psalm 24

O GOD, Lord and Ruler of the whole world, let it please thee of thy good grace to dwell among us, and make us participant of all thy celestial blessings, that we, being strengthened by thy power, may obtain victory over all our enemies, in the name of thy Son, Jesus Christ. Amen.

Psalm 25

GOOD AND GRACIOUS GOD, who desirest nothing but the health and salvation of them that trust in thee, extend thy goodness and infinite mercies upon us thy poor servants, and put away all our iniquities, that we, being governed by thy Holy Spirit, may walk uprightly in thy holy commandments, without any wavering; that in the end we may enjoy the bliss obtained for us by thy Son, Christ Jesus. AMEN.

Psalm 26

O LORD, OUR RIGHTEOUS JUDGE, since it has pleased thee to choose us for thine own people, and to separate us from the company of the ungodly, deliver us from their calumnies and oppressions, and grant that we, continually abiding in thy church, and living in all purity and uprightness, may ever magnify thy holy name, in thy holy congregations, through Jesus Christ, thy Son, our Saviour. Amen.

Psalm 27

FATHER OF LIGHT and fountain of all goodness, be helpful unto us in time of our affliction: and when we are in greatest danger, hide not thy face from us; yea, whatsoever thing fall unto us, strengthen our hearts, that we may have a continual hope of all the good things, which thou hast promised to us, through Jesus Christ our Lord. Amen.

Psalm 28

O GOD FULL OF ALL CONSOLATION, who lovest equity, and detestest all hypocrisy and iniquity, destroy the enterprises of all them that seek our destruction. Be thou the strength and buckler of all those that trust in thee, that in all spiritual joy, we may sing praises to the forthsetting of thy glory, through Christ our Lord. AMEN.

Psalm 29

MIGHTY LORD, to whom all glory and honour do justly appertain, since it hath pleased thee to make us understand thy will by thy holy Word, grant likewise that we may receive the same with all reverence, and that we may have a feeling of the force and strength thereof that thereby we may be reformed in all holiness of life, that in the end we may enjoy the heritage promised to all them, that are adopted in thy well-beloved Son, Christ Jesus. AMEN.

Psalm 30

O GOD, Deliverer of all them that call upon thee in their adversity, deliver us from the malice of our enemies: and suffer not that in time of prosperity we abuse thy benefits, but that we may give over ourselves to the magnifying and praising of thy holy name through Jesus Christ. AMEN.

Psalm 31

ETERNAL GOD, who knowest our weakness and infirmities, show thyself our protector and defender, and destroy the counsels of all them that devise any mischief against us, thy poor servants; and give unto us those good gifts, which thou hast promised to reserve to all them that fear and worship thee, through Jesus Christ thy Son. AMEN.

Psalm 32

MERCIFUL FATHER, who desirest not the death, but rather the life and amendment, of the sinner, extend thy grace, mercy and goodness to us, and bury all our iniquities, that, being guarded with thy goodness, we may rejoice in thee, living in all uprightness, as we are instructed by thy Son, Jesus Christ. AMEN.

Psalm 33

O ETERNAL GOD, grant unto us that thy holy name may always be magnified among us; and that thy mighty and holy Word be so imprinted in our hearts, that we undertake nothing against thy godly will; to the intent that we continually depend on thy good providence, and be replenished with that joy that shall uphold our hope of all those good things which thou hast promised to us through Jesus Christ. AMEN.

Psalm 34

HEAVENLY FATHER, who makest all creatures, yea, the very Angels themselves, for thy wealth, let us have a feeling of thy mercy and goodness, that we, giving ourselves to all good works, may live peaceably with our brethren; that in the end we may be found holy and irreprovable before the great judge, Jesus Christ our Saviour. AMEN.

Psalm 35

LORD GOD, who knowest the power of them that lift themselves against us, defend and assist our cause, to the intent that the proud wicked blaspheme not thy most holy name, as though thou wert not mighty enough to deliver us from their violence. And grant that we, abiding with thee in all truth and faithfulness, may render to thee perpetual praises, through Jesus Christ our Saviour. AMEN.

Psalm 36

O RIGHTEOUS FATHER, whom the world knoweth not, imprint thy fear in our hearts, which may chase away all wickedness and iniquity from us. Prepare our hearts to all good works, that we, depending on thy providence, and living under the shadow of thy wings, may be replenished with the abundance of thy blessings, promised and prepared for all those whom thou hast given to Jesus Christ thy Son. AMEN.

Psalm 37

O GOD, the Author and Fountain of all goodness, who governest the whole world by thy marvellous wisdom, suffer not that we be any wise moved with the prosperous success of the ungodly; but that we may the rather give ourselves wholly to thy service, and continual meditation on thy holy law; that in the end we may effectually find thee to be our Saviour and Redeemer, when thou shalt come to judge the whole world, through thy well-beloved Son, Christ Jesus. AMEN.

Psalm 38

O LORD, who art a just Judge, in respect of the just occasion of thy anger conceived against us by reason of our grievous sins daily committed against thy holy Majesty: yet we beseech thee that thou wilt turn away thy fury and thy anger from us, lest thereby we be consumed and brought to naught. Deliver us from all our enemies, and show thyself to have care of our health and salvation, through Jesus Christ, thy Son, our Lord. AMEN.

Psalm 39

ALMIGHTY GOD, of whom proceedeth all our sufficiency, assist us by thy Holy Spirit that we neither think nor do anything that is against thy holy will. Hear our prayers, defeat our enemies, and comfort us by the self-same Spirit, that we may continually feel thy fatherly favour and goodwill which thou showest to thy own children, through Jesus Christ, thy Son. AMEN.

Psalm 40

O LORD, who by thy providence dost guide and govern all things, and who hast sent to us thy well-beloved Son, to deliver us from sin and death, by the oblation of his body on the Cross, grant that we may continually acknowledge this thy great and inestimable benefit, and that we may ever have our hearts and mouths open to proclaim thy praises among all men, by thy self-same Son, Jesus Christ, our Saviour. AMEN.[1]

---

[1] The French original of 1567 reads: 'Seigneur, qui par ta providence conduis et gouvernes toutes choses, et qui nous as envoyé ton Fils bien aimé pour nous délivrer de

Psalm 41

O GOD OF ALL CONSOLATION, grant of thy infinite goodness that those fatherly chastisements which thou layest upon us may be so profitable unto us that our enemies thereby have no occasion of triumphing over us; but that they may be ashamed and confounded, and we may be inflamed by thy Holy Spirit to sing praises unto thee perpetually through Jesus Christ thy Son, our Saviour. AMEN.

---

péché et de la mort par le sacrifice de son corps: fay que nous recognoissons tousieurs ce benefice inestimable et qu'ayons incessamment la bouche ouverte pour annoncer tes louanges à un chacun par iceluy ton Fils Jesus Christ nostre Seigneur. Amen.'

Psalm 42

HEAVENLY FATHER, who at all times exercisest thy poor flock with diverse afflictions, assist us and deliver us from the troubles that are falling on us, that the wicked and proud contemners may have no cause to think that in vain we depend upon thee, but that they may be compelled to understand that thou art the strength and fortress of all them that love and honour thee in thy Son, Jesus Christ. AMEN.

Psalm 43

ETERNAL GOD, who hast created us to glorify thy holy name, turn away thine anger from us, and take our cause into thy own hand against them that oppress us.

Show us thy favour and fulfil thy promises, that we may render and give unto thee, in thy holy congregation, all honour and glory, through thy dear Son, Jesus Christ. AMEN.

Psalm 44

FATHER OF ALL MERCY, who did enter into covenant with our forefathers, which thou hast ratified by thy Son, Jesus Christ, deliver us from those tyrants who cruelly pursue us, to the intent that they may understand that thou never leavest destitute them that trust in thy goodness, and who render unto thee continually due honour and reverence, through Jesus Christ, thy Son. AMEN.

Psalm 45

GOOD LORD, AND GOD ALMIGHTY, who for the fulfilling of thy holy promises, hast sent unto us thy dear Son, our King and Redeemer, grant that we so order ourselves, under the obedience of thy holy Word, that we may renounce ourselves and all our carnal affections; and that we may be an occasion to all people to celebrate thy holy name throughout the whole earth, and that through the self-same Jesus Christ, our only Saviour. AMEN.

Psalm 46

O LORD, the only refuge and strength of all them who put their trust in thee, we beseech thee of thy goodness to fortify us, and to destroy the devices of the wicked in such sort that we may live in quietness of spirit; that we may serve and honour thee all the days of our life, through Jesus Christ, thy Son. AMEN.

Psalm 47

O LORD GOD, King of Kings, who holdest all nations under thy subjection, deliver us out of the danger of those that seek our overthrow and destruction, to the intent that all men may know thy care and love which thou hast of thy heritage, that we may sing psalms to thee, through Jesus Christ, our Lord. AMEN.

Psalm 48

O GOD, the only deliverer of thy church, who showest forth continually so many evident signs of thy favour which thou bearest unto us, in casting down our adversaries, and bringing to naught all their forces; continue thy goodwill toward us, to the intent that we, being in safeguard under thy holy protection, may ever have occasion to render thanks, honour, and praise unto thee, through Jesus Christ, thy Son. AMEN.

Psalm 49

HEAVENLY FATHER, conserver of all mankind, suffer us never to be so entangled with earthly and corruptible things, wherein the children of this world put their trust and assurance, that we fail to acknowledge at all times our own weakness and miseries, lest through our unthankfulness we be justly spoiled of the fruit of that hope which thy children have in thee only, through Jesus Christ. AMEN.

Psalm 50

O LORD, the just Judge of all the world, who hast given us thy holy law to govern us after thy holy will, grant us of thy grace that we, renouncing all impiety and hypocrisy, may serve thee in spirit and verity, may call upon thee in all our necessities, and magnify thy holy Name, until thy salvation appear which thou hast promised unto us, by thy dear Son, Jesus Christ. AMEN.

Psalm 51

FATHER OF ALL MERCIES, who delightest not in the death of a sinner, have
compassion upon us, and wash us from all
our sins that we have committed against
thy holy Majesty since the time we first
came into this world. Create in us a clean
heart, and strengthen us continually with
the power of thy Holy Spirit, that we,
being truly consecrated to thy service, may
set forth thy praises, through Jesus Christ,
our Saviour. AMEN.

Psalm 52

O GOD MOST HOLY, grant us of thy
goodness that, being armed with thy
grace, we may divert and turn from men
replete with malice and deceit. Destroy

them utterly, that they may be rooted out and severed from among the living, that, when the just shall see these things come to pass, they may fear and rejoice in thee as becometh thy children, and may render and give unto thee perpetual praises and thanks, through Jesus Christ, thy Son. AMEN.

Psalm 53

O LORD GOD, the fountain of all justice, who abhorrest all impiety and wickedness, mortify by the power of thy Holy Spirit all corruptions that naturally dwell in us, and deliver us from all errors and iniquities; to the intent that we be not wrapped under the destruction and just punishment of the mockers of thy holy Word and despisers of the good gifts which thou hast given to us in thy Son, Jesus Christ, our only Saviour and Redeemer. AMEN.

Psalm 54

ALMIGHTY GOD AND HEAVENLY FATHER, who never leavest destitute those that put their trust and confidence in thee, so take our cause into thy own hand against all our enemies, who are so terrible and so fearful, that they may understand that it is against thee that they enterprise. Declare also thy mercies toward them that help us, to the intent that we have continually occasion to offer up to thee sacrifice of thanksgiving, through Jesus Christ, our Lord and Saviour. AMEN.

Psalm 55

O FATHER, righteous in all thy judgments, who, for the trial of our patience, dost suffer us to be afflicted both within and without: deliver us from all our enemies. Discover the craft and hypocrisy of all those who, by their fair and sweet words, go about to suppress us. Stop their false tongues, shorten the course of their life, and make it known unto them that thou hast delight in none but in those who trust in thee, through Jesus Christ, thy dear Son. AMEN.

Psalm 56

TRUE AND EVER-LIVING GOD, the only help and support of all thy poor afflicted people, destroy the enterprise of all our enemies, and let all that trust in thy promises feel thy fatherly goodness. Despise not our prayers, but be helpful to us in the time of our troubles, that we, having assurance of thy favour, need not regard the force of our enemies, but may render unto thee continual praises for delivering us out of all dangers, through Jesus Christ, thy dear Son. AMEN.

Psalm 57

GOOD AND GRACIOUS GOD, who hast willed us to walk before thee in all sincerity and cleanness of life, grant that those wicked, crafty, and malicious tyrants have no power to annoy us, according to their will; but that, they being rooted out of the number of the living, we may remain as fruitful trees in thy house, through the good hope we have in thee, and in thy Son, Christ Jesus our Lord. AMEN.

Psalm 58

MERCIFUL LORD, the righteous Judge of the world, who knowest the malice and cruelty of the enemies of thy church, repress their blasphemies, cast down their fierce looks, and utterly confound them, that the godly, seeing the fearful vengeance that thou takest upon thy enemies, may be more and more moved to praise thy righteousness and goodness, and may praise thy holy name, through Jesus Christ, our Saviour. AMEN.

Psalm 59

ETERNAL GOD, who delightest in the innocence and uprightness of those that serve thee with their whole heart, cast down our enemies who mock thy holy providence, and who do nothing but devise our destruction. Destroy their enterprises and spoil them of their power, to the intent they may know that thou bearest rule in thy church, and showest mercy to all them that put their trust in thee, through Jesus Christ thy Son. AMEN.

Psalm 60

O LORD GOD, who desirest not the death, but rather the conversion, of poor sinners, handle us not according to the rigour of thy justice, but by thy mighty power put back all them that rise against us; that we, putting our whole trust in thee only, may obtain victory, and thereby render thee hearty thanks, through thy dear Son, Jesus Christ, our Lord and Saviour. AMEN.

Psalm 61

A LMIGHTY GOD, the help and defence of all them that fear thee, grant that we may securely live under the safeguard and protection of thy well-beloved Son, Jesus Christ. Grant also that his kingdom, by thy great power, may prosper and be advanced daily more and more; and that we, being settled upon thy promises, may render unto thee the sacrifice of praise and thanksgiving, both now and evermore. AMEN.

Psalm 62

ETERNAL GOD, who art the only glory and hope of thy children, assist us ever in time of our troubles, and deliver us from the troops of all our enemies. Show unto them that all is but vanity, and that what they account their great riches and treasure is nothing, seeing there is no health for any but those that trust thy goodness and mercy, which thou hast declared and made manifest to us in thy dear Son, Jesus Christ. AMEN.

Psalm 63

O LOVING GOD, who hast promised to be in the midst of those that call upon thee in verity, grant unto us that we may so call upon thee in open assembly that, being under thy protection, we may find thy grace and fatherly favour more and more; so that under the kingdom of thy Son, Christ Jesus, we may obtain full victory over all them that trouble us. Amen.

Psalm 64

ETERNAL AND EVER-LIVING GOD, who confoundest the wise of the world in their own wisdom, withdraw us from the company of the wicked, and out of the society of the ungodly, who study continually to calumniate thy poor servants and them that trust in thee. Deliver us from the snares they lay for us, so that we may have cause daily to glorify thy goodness, which thou makest us to feel through thy well-beloved Son, Jesus Christ. AMEN.

Psalm 65

FAVOURABLE AND MOST MERCIFUL FATHER, who hast elected and placed us in thy church, grant that we may continually acknowledge this thine inestimable benefit; that, ever dependent upon thy power and goodness, we regard not our adversaries, but may live in quietness, always ready to sing thy praises, through Jesus Christ, thy Son. AMEN.

Psalm 66

O LORD, to whom all glory and honour do appertain, make thy marvellous works known throughout the whole earth, so that the force of thy power may bring down thy enemies and ours. Further grant to us that we may be so settled by the afflictions which thou sendest unto us that we never cease to praise thy mercy and goodness, which is abundantly shown forth to us in thy dear Son, Jesus Christ, our Redeemer. AMEN.

Psalm 67

E TERNAL GOD, the Father of all lights, without the knowledge of whom we are more miserable than the very brute beasts, extend thy blessing over us, and make thy most holy name known throughout the whole earth, that thou mayest be worshipped of all people and nations; so that all men, feeling thy merciful benediction, may walk in thy fear, as we are taught by Jesus Christ, thy Son. AMEN.

Psalm 68

MOST POWERFUL GOD OF HOSTS, who maintainest and keepest all them that trust in thee, bend forth thine invincible force to destroy our enemies; make feeble the strength of the proud; turn our trouble into prosperity, and grant that in the midst of our assemblies the praise of thy holy name may be so celebrated as shall be most agreeable to thy Word, proclaimed by thy Son, Jesus Christ. AMEN.

Psalm 69

ETERNAL FATHER, and God of all consolation, who to make satisfaction for our sins didst cast down thy only Son to extreme pains and anguish, and hast ordained thy church to pass by the same way of affliction, we beseech thee most fervently that, forasmuch as we are destitute of all help of men, we may so much the more be assured of thy mercy and goodness, that we may praise the same before all creatures, both now and evermore. AMEN.

Psalm 70

CELESTIAL AND HEAVENLY FATHER, the protector and defender of all them that put their confidence in thee, haste thee to help us, and destroy the counsels of all them that scorn us, because we trust in thy goodness. Grant that all those that seek thee with their whole heart, and call upon thee in spirit and verity, may have continually new occasion to praise and magnify thy holy name, through Jesus Christ, our Saviour. AMEN.

Psalm 71

CELESTIAL AND MOST MIGHTY GOD, who art our continual helper, let not thy goodness and clemency be far from us; grant of thy sovereign justice that such as seek our destruction may be confounded, and be compelled to understand that there is not a God like unto thee. Deliver us out of all our troubles, and comfort thy poor afflicted ones, that we may have continual matter to sing psalms to thee, with thanks and praises agreeable thereto, through Jesus Christ our Saviour. AMEN.

Psalm 72

HEAVENLY FATHER, fountain of all our felicity, who knowest how unto this present hour we have been oppressed under the tyranny of Satan, enemy to all justice and righteousness, we beseech thee of thy great power that thou wouldst so order and establish the kingdom of thy Son Jesus Christ that he, by the sceptre of his Word, may so reign over us that we, renouncing the world and ourselves, may serve him in fear and humility for ever. AMEN.

Psalm 73

O SWEET AND GRACIOUS LORD, grant us of thy grace that we never be so envious of the prosperous estate of the ungodly that we decline from the right course of the godly, but that we may be more and more assured of thy goodness and providence, in such sort that our whole aim may be to be perpetually conjoined with thee, through thy only Son, Jesus Christ our Saviour. AMEN.

Psalm 74

FATHER OF MERCY, although thou hast just occasion to punish us, in respect that we have not made our profit of those benefits which thou hast poured forth upon us even unto this present hour, yet have regard to the glory of thy holy name, which is blasphemed by proud contemners and despisers thereof. Withdraw not thy favour from us, but remember the covenant made with our fathers of old, and strengthen us by thy adoption ratified in us, through Jesus Christ, thy Son. AMEN.

Psalm 75

O LORD, ruler and governor of the whole world, grant unto us that we praise thy holy name perpetually. Preserve thy poor church from destruction; repress the pride and boldness of her proud adversaries; and cast thine anger upon the despisers of thy blessed Word; to the intent that, when the ungodly are cast down and the godly exalted, everyone may render unto thee due honour, praise, and glory, through Jesus Christ, our Lord. AMEN.

Psalm 76

O LORD GOD, who hast manifested thyself to thy people Israel, but much more openly unto us by Jesus Christ thy Son, pour forth more and more thy favour and goodness upon us. Bruise down the force, and undo the counsels, of our adversaries, and deliver the poor afflicted ones out of their hands, that they may continually set forth thy praises; and that all the world may know that unto thee all kings, princes, yea, and all creatures owe honour and obedience. AMEN.

Psalm 77

ETERNAL GOD, the only refuge of comfortless creatures, hear our prayers and requests, and forget not to show thy mercy upon us. Lord, give us grace in such sort to acknowledge thy marvellous works which thou hast shown to thy people in times past, that we may be daily more and more confirmed in the assurance of thy goodness, by the which thou hast freely elected and adopted us in thy well-beloved Son, Jesus Christ. AMEN.

Psalm 78

O GOOD GOD, who through the multitude of thy benefits, heaped upon us, ceasest not to incite us to honour and serve thee, nevertheless our wicked nature

and unfaithfulness is such that we give not
that obedience which is thy due unto thee.
Yet we beseech thee that thou wilt not put
forth thy anger upon us, but put away all our
iniquities out of thy sight through thy mercy,
and have pity upon us, the poor sheep of thy
pasture who are redeemed by the blood of
thy Son, Christ Jesus. AMEN.

Psalm 79

O LORD, the protector and defender of
the poor and oppressed, although the
rage and fury of our enemies be such that
they never cease from continually torment-
ing us all manner of ways, and seek nothing
but our utter destruction, yet we beseech
thee to assist us, and turn away thine
anger that hangs over us, [turning it] upon

them that blaspheme thee, that all the world may understand that thou despisest not the complaints and sobs of them that call upon thee in truth and verity, in the name of Jesus Christ, thy Son. AMEN.

Psalm 80

ALMIGHTY GOD, who of thy goodness hast placed us in the sheepfold of thy Son, Jesus Christ, that we should be governed by him as the only Pastor and Bishop of our souls, turn not away thy favourable face from us but look down out of heaven and behold how these cruel tyrants continually seek our death and destruction. Pour out thy fury upon them, and defend us from all evils, that we may render thee perpetual praises, through the self-same Jesus Christ. AMEN.

Psalm 81

O HEAVENLY FATHER, who never ceasest to pour thy benefits upon thy children, although by our ingratitude we have often and many times provoked thy fury against us, yet, we pray thee, remember the covenant made with our fathers, that thou wouldst be their God and the God of their seed. Have pity upon us. Give us thy grace, that we may so walk before thee that we may be participant of thy heavenly felicity, through Jesus Christ our Lord. AMEN.

Psalm 82

E TERNAL GOD, to whom all power and empire appertain, grant of thy infinite goodness that those whom thou hast appointed rulers and governors over us may so discharge themselves of their duty and office that the glory of thy most holy name may be advanced, the godly may be maintained, the wicked punished, and the poor comforted, to the end that, leading a quiet and peaceable life under their government, we may render all honour and praise unto thee, through Jesus Christ our Lord. AMEN.

Psalm 83

O MIGHTY GOD, the only true comforter of the afflicted poor, behold the threatenings and villanies of thine enemies and ours, who puff up themselves in great pride, utterly to destroy thy church. Repress them, O Lord, and destroy their enterprises. Confound them and make them contemptible, and cast them down by thy power, so that all may know that it is to thee only all reverence and honour appertain, through Jesus Christ, thy Son, our Lord and Saviour. Amen.

Psalm 84

MOST MERCIFUL AND HEAVENLY FATHER, without the knowledge of whom we can in no wise attain to life everlasting or eternal salvation, seeing it hath pleased thee of thy mercy, good and gracious God, to grant us liberty to convene ourselves together, to invocate and call upon thy most holy Name, and to hear and embrace wholesome and sound doctrine, as out of thine own mouth, continue, of thine own goodness, according to thy wonted mercy, this thy heavenly favour toward us and our posterity; and defend the cause of all those who walk before thy holy Majesty in innocency and cleanness of life, that we may be encouraged daily more and more to put our whole trust and confidence in thee; and that through the merits of Jesus Christ, thy dear and only Son, our Saviour. AMEN.

Psalm 85

O LORD, who never leavest imperfect that which thou hast begun, although our wickedness and unthankfulness deserve that we should be deprived of all thy benefits, nevertheless we beseech thee of thy great mercy to cast away our sins; and grant that we may fear and serve thee in such sort that thou maintain us in peace and tranquillity, through Jesus Christ our Lord. AMEN.

Psalm 86

ETERNAL GOD, the only relief of those who put their trust in thee, hear our prayers, and grant that, as hitherto thou hast been blasphemed and dishonoured even unto this present, so henceforth thou mayest be praised of all nations. And continue in such sort thy favour toward us, that all those who hate us may be ashamed of themselves, seeing that thou leavest not destitute those who serve and honour thee; through Jesus Christ, thy Son, our Lord and Saviour. AMEN.

Psalm 87

O LORD GOD, the only founder of thy church, augment and increase daily the number of the faithful by the preaching of thy holy Evangel, that the darkness of ignorance may be chased out of the world, and that thy name may be known over all. May all men resort out of all parts to render themselves under the obedience of thy Word, and may they reverence thee with their whole hearts, through Jesus Christ, our Lord. AMEN.

Psalm 88

ETERNAL FATHER who, for our great good, dost cast us into many calamities and miseries, despise not our prayers, lest in thy fury thou dost reject and cast us clean away. Have pity on us thy poor servants, who call daily upon thee, and replenish us with thy grace, to the intent that all those in whose eyes we are contemptible and despised may understand that yet thou lovest us, in thy well-beloved Son, Jesus Christ. AMEN.

Psalm 89

O GOD ONLY WISE AND GOOD, who never ceasest to show unto thine elect how greatly thou lovest and favourest them, but chiefly when thou gavest unto us a King and Saviour, Jesus Christ, thy only Son, to assure us of the truth of thy promises; we beseech thee, grant us thy grace to render unto him such obedience that we may in the end enjoy the fruit of our faith, that is, the salvation of our souls. AMEN.

Psalm 90

ETERNAL GOD, the only refuge of the afflicted, seeing that the shortness of this present life admonishes us to turn ourselves away from earthly things and to have our meditation on heavenly matters, grant unto us that we may employ our whole life on the consideration of thy mercy and goodness; and that thine anger may be so turned from us that we may have continually wherewith to rejoice in thee, through Jesus Christ, our Lord. AMEN.

Psalm 91

ETERNAL GOD, who makest all things to turn for the best to them that love thee, and who preservest and keepest all those who commit themselves to thy protection, grant us of thy bountiful grace that we may continually call upon thee with our whole hearts, that, being delivered from all dangers, we may in the end enjoy that salvation which is acquired for us by Jesus Christ, thine only Son, our Saviour. AMEN.

Psalm 92

MERCIFUL LORD, in the knowledge of whom lies life eternal, replenish us with thy grace and Holy Spirit, that we, considering thy marvellous works, which the wicked despise, may give ourselves continually to sanctify thy holy Name; and that we may so grow in all good virtues that, being true members of thy church, we may in the end see the destruction of thine enemies and ours, when thou shalt deliver all them who put their trust in thee, through Jesus Christ, thy only Son. AMEN.

Psalm 93

MOST POTENT KING OF KINGS AND LORD OF LORDS, whose glory is incomprehensible, whose majesty is infinite, and whose power is incomparable, maintain thy servants in quietness; and grant that we may be so settled on the certainty of thy promises that, whatsoever thing come upon us, we may abide firm in thy faith, and may live uprightly and without reproach in the midst of thy church, which Jesus Christ thy Son hath bought with his precious blood. AMEN.

Psalm 94

JUST AND RIGHTEOUS JUDGE of all the world, who knowest how fierce and cruel those are that lift up themselves against us, repress, by thy invincible power, their undaunted rage; and grant us that we make profit out of all the calamities that fall upon us. Dispose the estate of this world in such order that everyone may renounce wicked ways and follow thee; and that the more earnestly because thou showest thyself a just and righteous God, through our Lord and Saviour, Christ Jesus. AMEN.

Psalm 95

O LORD, the only protector and stay of all thine, who guidest thy children as the sheep of thy fold, extend thy goodness to us, and so sustain our hearts, which by nature are harder than any flint, that we be not hardened or obstinate through any incredulity against thy holy Word, but that we may serve thee in true and living faith, so that in the end we may enter into thy heavenly rest, through Jesus Christ our Lord. AMEN.

Psalm 96

O GOOD LORD, who willest all people to be saved and to come to the knowledge of thy verity, show thy power and excellent Majesty unto the whole world, that everyone may sing thy praises, yea, and show forth thy salvation, which thou hast promised to all them that dedicate themselves to thy service; that thou mayest be praised in all thy creatures, by means of Jesus Christ thy Son. AMEN.

Psalm 97

O LORD, unto whom all glory and honour do appertain, replenish us with spiritual joy; grant that, all idolatry and superstition being put away, the whole world may be so enlightened with the light of thy holy Word, that every man may give over himself to a perpetual praising of thy holy Name, and may give unto thee most hearty thanks for all the benefits which we continually receive at thy hand, through Jesus Christ thy Son. AMEN.

Psalm 98

ALMIGHTY AND EVERLASTING, who hast wrought the redemption of man after a marvellous manner, in sending thine only Son to fulfil the promises made unto our

fathers, open up more and more the knowledge of that salvation, that in all places of
the earth thy truth and power may be made
known; to the intent that all nations may
praise, honour, and glorify thee through the
self-same Son, Jesus Christ. AMEN.

Psalm 99

O HEAVENLY FATHER, worthy of all
praises, continue thy favour and
goodwill toward us, thy poor servants, and,
by the force of that covenant which thou
hast contracted with our forefathers, grant
that we may safely live under thy safeguard
and protection, that we may continually
more and more have a feeling of the fruit
of that adoption whereof thou hast made us
participant, through Jesus Christ thy Son,
our Lord. AMEN.

Psalm 100

O LORD, the plentiful store of all happiness, since it has pleased thee of thy free mercy and goodness to choose us for thy own heritage, and to regenerate us spiritually, entertain us under thy wings unto the end; and grant that we may daily grow in the knowledge of thy goodness, truth, and mercy, which thou hast manifested unto us, through our Redeemer and Saviour, Jesus Christ. AMEN.

Psalm 101

ETERNAL GOD, under whose power are all those whom thou hast placed as rulers and superiors over us, let it please thee so to enlighten the hearts of all judges and magistrates, whom thou hast given us, that without respect of persons they may maintain the righteous and punish the wicked; to the intent that, under their protection, we may lead a quiet and peaceable life according to the instruction given us by Jesus Christ thy Son, our only Saviour and Redeemer. AMEN.

Psalm 102

O GOD, the only Founder and Restorer of thy church, hearken unto the prayers and sobs of us thy poor children, who sorrow for the desolation of the same, seeking to thee continually for her; earnestly beseeching thee to look down out of heaven, see her misery, and deliver her out of captivity and from all oppression, that we in joyfulness of heart may praise and magnify thy holy name, through our Redeemer and Saviour, Jesus Christ. AMEN.

Psalm 103

CELESTIAL FATHER, who at all times hast shown thy singular favour and goodness toward all them that fear thee, look not upon the multitude of our iniquities wherewith we offend thee, seeing the great fragility and weakness which are in us. But remember the covenant which thou hast made with our fathers, and ratified in thy Son Christ Jesus, that by virtue thereof we may assure ourselves of eternal salvation, that we with the angels may praise and glorify thee for ever and ever. AMEN.

Psalm 104

O DEAR FATHER, whose providence extendeth over all thy creatures, in such sort that thy marvellous wisdom is uttered through them all: grant that we may exalt thy glory, and sing praises and psalms to the forthsetting and magnifying of the same; to the intent, that, the wicked being banished from off the earth, we may rejoice in thee, and in the end may be participant of that eternal life and felicity, which are promised unto us, through Jesus Christ thy Son. AMEN.

Psalm 105

O LORD, only just and righteous, who from among all the nations of the world hast chosen thy church for the better manifesting of thy blessed name in her, and hast received us of thy free mercy in that holy society, grant that we may have a perfect feeling of the sweetness of thy mercies, and assist us in the time of our troubles, seeing we call upon thee and put our whole trust in thee only. Suffer not, O Lord, that we become unthankful for the great benefits which thou givest unto us; but rather that we may magnify the excellency of thy power and goodness, which thou hast declared unto us, in Jesus Christ. AMEN.

Psalm 106

FATHER most pitiful and full of mercy, although through our unthankfulness and wickedness we cease not to provoke thee to wrath and anger against us by loosing the bridle to all our corrupt affections, nevertheless, since it hath pleased thee to admit us into the sacred covenant which thou hast made with our fathers, we beseech thee not to punish us according to the rigour of thy justice, but deliver us from all trouble, that we may with thanksgiving sing praises to thy holy Name, through Jesus Christ our only Saviour. AMEN.

Psalm 107

O LORD OF MERCY, and full of all benignity, who chastisest men in diverse sorts to make them return unto thee, suffer not, O Father, that we, through our unthankfulness, forget thine inestimable benefits, and the most singular deliverances which thou hast bestowed on us from day to day; but grant, that we may continually be careful and mindful to consider all the days of our lives thy gifts incomparable, which thou ever givest to us, through Jesus Christ. AMEN.

Psalm 108[1]

O LORD OF MERCY, and full of all benignity, who chastisest men in diverse sorts to make them return unto thee: Suffer not, O Father, that we, through our unthankfulness, forget thine inestimable benefits, and the most singular deliverances which thou hast bestowed on us from day to day; but grant, that we may continually be careful and mindful to consider all the days of our lives thy gifts incomparable, which thou ever givest to us through our Redeemer and Saviour, Jesus Christ. AMEN.

[1] In the 1595 Scottish Psalter, this collect is almost identical with the foregoing, the only difference occurring at the conclusion of the prayer.

Psalm 109

O LORD, on whom only we repose, and in whom only we rejoice, behold the multitude, yea, and the malice and cruelty of those that blaspheme and bend themselves against us. Destroy their enterprises and undo their wicked counsels. Turn their cursings into blessings, to the intent that we may have continual occasion to praise and magnify thy name in midst of thy church, the spouse of thy only Son, our Lord Jesus Christ. AMEN.

Psalm 110

ETERNAL GOD, who hast appointed thine only Son to be our King and Priest, that we might be sanctified by the sacrifice of his body upon the Cross, grant that we may be so participant of his benefits that we may renounce our own selves, and serve him in all holiness and purity of life, and may offer up spiritual sacrifices that may be pleasant and acceptable unto thee, through the self-same Jesus Christ. AMEN.

Psalm 111

MOST PITIFUL AND LOVING FATHER, who ceasest not, by all means and ways, to draw us to love, fear, and obey thee, and to keep thy holy statutes and commandments, behold not, O our gracious God, our vanity and unthankfulness, but have regard unto thy promises and look unto the covenant which thou hast made with us who walk in thy fear. And suffer us never to be spoiled of the inestimable fruit of the redemption, purchased by the blood of thy dear Son, Jesus Christ, our Redeemer and only Saviour. AMEN.

Psalm 112

MOST LOVING FATHER, without whose blessing we are altogether poor and miserable creatures, imprint thy holy Word on all our hearts, in such sort that our whole pleasure and delight may be to serve thee in all fear and reverence. Grant that we may be so merciful towards our poor neighbours that we may also have a sure feeling of thy mercy and goodness, when thou shalt come to judge the world by him whom thou hast ordained to be our Lord and Sovereign, Jesus Christ. AMEN.

Psalm 113

O THOU GOOD LORD, who only art worthy of all glory and majesty, and who takest pleasure in things vile and contemptible in the sight of the world, we beseech thee so to mortify and illuminate our hearts and wills that, all obstinacy and pride being set apart, we may humbly submit ourselves under the obedience of thy holy Word; that we, bringing forth the fruits of all good works, may sing praises to thee perpetually, through Jesus Christ, our only Saviour. AMEN.

Psalm 114

A LMIGHTY GOD, the only deliverer of poor and miserable creatures, who hast delivered us from the servitude of sin and from the tyranny of Satan by means of thy Son Jesus Christ, the Saviour of the world, grant unto us that we, acknowledging so great and mighty deliverances, may walk safely under thy government in all holiness of life, until we attain to the full possession of the true land of the living, where we may continually praise thee. AMEN.

Psalm 115

O LORD OF ALL CONSOLATION AND COMFORT, look down upon thy church oppressed by her enemies and deliver her for the glory of thy holy name, that the ungodly may be kept from blaspheming thee. Destroy this filthy idolatry which overruns the whole world. Suffer not, good God, that we be exposed to the angry will of our enemies; that we, in despite of them, being maintained by thee, may bless and glorify thee, both now and evermore. AMEN.

Psalm 116

ALMIGHTY GOD, the only helper and deliverer of all them that love and honour thee, extend thy mercy and goodness to help us thy children, as often as we call upon thee in our afflictions. Turn our sorrows into joys, and imprint a true faith in our hearts, so that we may be able to give a sound confession thereof before all men; and that we may so profit by thy rod which thou layest on us that we may never cease to celebrate and invoke thy holy Name before all men, through Jesus Christ our Lord. AMEN.

Psalm 117

O GOOD LORD, unto whom appertains all glory and magnificence, grant unto us that by the preaching of thy holy Evangel thou mayest be acknowledged throughout the whole earth; so that all nations may have a perfect feeling of thy mercies, and that thy faithfulness may be more and more manifested, through Christ Jesus, thy Son. AMEN.

Psalm 118

O LOVING AND MERCIFUL FATHER, who never leavest them that put their trust in thee, and who, as a father, chastisest thy children for their own health, grant that we may be built as lively stones upon Jesus Christ, the true and only foundation of the church; that forasmuch as he was rejected and despised of men, we may acknowledge him always for our King and Saviour; that we may for ever enjoy the fruit of thy mercy and goodness. AMEN.

Psalm 119

MOST MERCIFUL GOD, Author of all good things, who hast given thy holy commandments unto us, whereby we should direct our life, imprint them in our hearts by thy Holy Spirit; and grant that we may so renounce all our fleshly desires, and all the vanities of this world, that our whole pleasure and delight may be in thy law; that we, being always governed by thy holy Word, may in the end attain to that eternal salvation which thou hast promised, through Christ Jesus, thy Son. AMEN.

Psalm 120

MOST LOVING AND MERCIFUL FATHER, the defender and protector of all thy servants, deliver us from the deceits and calumnies of our enemies; repress their rage and fury, and strengthen us in the midst of all our tribulations and afflictions, that we may so live among infidels that we may never cease to serve and honour thee with such service as shall be acceptable and pleasant unto thee, and that through the mediation and intercession of Jesus Christ, thy Son. AMEN.

Psalm 121

O HEAVENLY FATHER, Creator of heaven and earth, who hast taken us into thy protection, suffer not our afflictions so to overcome us that we cast off all confidence in thee; but rather prosper and conduct all our enterprises, and give a happy end and issue to all our businesses, that we may continually be more and more assured that we are of the number of them whom thou hast chosen to salvation, through Jesus Christ, thy Son. AMEN.

Psalm 122

O ETERNAL GOD, the only founder and keeper of thy church, seeing that, contrary to all worldly judgment and opinion, thou dost daily augment the number of thy own, grant that we, being placed under the government of Jesus Christ, the only Chief and Head thereof, may be comforted by thy most holy Word, and strengthened and confirmed by thy Sacraments; to the intent that we all, with one heart and mouth, may glorify thee, edifying one another in holiness of life and godly conversation. AMEN.

Psalm 123

O GRACIOUS FATHER, the only refuge and support of the afflicted poor, thou seest the rage of our enemies who use all means to destroy us; thou knowest how we are disdained and lightly esteemed by the proud and mighty of the world. Therefore, having this only remedy, we lift up our eyes to thee, beseeching thee to have pity and compassion on us, and that for the sake of Jesus Christ, thy Son. AMEN.

Psalm 124

ALMIGHTY GOD, AND MERCIFUL FATHER, thou seest the multitude, the force, and the exceeding rage of our enemies to be so great that they would devour and tear us in pieces if thy bountiful mercy did not relieve and succour us. But, seeing their craft and fury increase and grow from day to day, declare thou thyself to be our defender and protector; that we, escaping their gins and snares, may give ourselves wholly to praising and magnifying thy most holy and blessed Name, and that through Jesus Christ, thy dear Son, our only Lord and Saviour. AMEN.

Psalm 125

O MIGHTY KING AND LORD, the rock and fortress of all them that put their trust in thee, undo the force and break down the pride of them that afflict thy poor church, and suffer not the simple ones to be overthrown by them, but confirm such as Mount Sion, that they may abide in the new Jerusalem, which is Christ's church. Suffer us not to shake hands with unrighteousness, but let peace be upon Israel, who walk not after the flesh but after the Spirit, through the self-same Jesus Christ. AMEN.

Psalm 126

E TERNAL FATHER, the only true God, and deliverer of poor captives and prisoners, we beseech thee of thy plentiful bounty to relieve us from the bondage of our adversaries, that we, passing through the miseries and calamities of this troublesome world, may in the end enjoy the fruit of our faith which is the salvation of our souls, bought by the blood of thy dear Son, Christ Jesus. AMEN.

Psalm 127

ETERNAL AND ALMIGHTY GOD, who by thy providence dost conduct and govern all creatures in this world, suffer us not to enterprise anything but what is agreeable to thy will and pleasure, that we, altogether discontented with ourselves, may wholly depend upon thy blessing; and that our only care may be that thou mayest be glorified in us and our posterity, through Jesus Christ, thy Son. AMEN.

Psalm 128

GRACIOUS LORD, who art the well-spring of all felicity, grant unto us that we may always fear thee, and walk in thy ways. Bless us and all ours, that it may be well with us and all who pertain to us; that we may see many generations and children of faith; and that we may see peace upon Israel, and so may glorify thee all the days of our lives, through Jesus Christ, thy Son. AMEN.

Psalm 129

ETERNAL GOD, who hast at all times shown forth the great care thou hast of thy church and thy poor servants, assist us with thy favour and grace, in such sort that we may overthrow all the enterprises of our enemies, that, they being confounded and put back with shame, we may in all safety and quietness praise and glorify thy holy name, all the days of our life, through Jesus Christ, our Lord and only Saviour. AMEN.

Psalm 130

PITIFUL FATHER, who art full of mercy, who never rejectest the prayers of them that call upon thee in truth and verity, have mercy upon us, and destroy the multitude of our iniquities, according to the truth of thy promises which thou hast promised unto us and wherein we repose our whole confidence, according as we are taught by the Word of thy Son, our only Saviour. AMEN.

Psalm 131

MIGHTY LORD, who resistest the proud and givest strength to the humble ones, suffer not that we lift up ourselves in any proud opinion or conceit of ourselves in any good thing; but grant that we may confess humbly before thy Divine Majesty without excusing ourselves. And grant that we may mortify ourselves daily more and more, in such sort that in all our doings we may continually feel thy fatherly favour, mercy, and assistance, through Jesus Christ, thy Son. AMEN.

Psalm 132

O LOVING FATHER, who by thine oath hast promised unto us a Saviour, Jesus Christ, thy Son, thou hast not deceived us, but hast given him unto us, as thy Word has declared, and by thy sacraments thou hast confirmed. Yea, he hath further promised unto us that he will abide with us until the consummation of the world. Therefore, dear Father, we beseech thee that thou wilt bless us in all our turns, govern us, and replenish us with joy. Let thy crown and kingdom abide above us, and preserve us in peace, through the same Jesus Christ, thy Son. AMEN.

Psalm 133

GRACIOUS LORD, who art not the God of confusion or discord, but the God of concord and of peace, join our hearts and affections in such sort together that we may walk in thy house as brethren, in brotherly charity and love, and as members of the body of Christ. Let the oil of sanctification, that is, thy Holy Spirit, inflame us, and the dew of thy blessing continually fall upon us, that we may obtain life eternal through the same Jesus Christ. Amen.

Psalm 134

CREATOR OF HEAVEN AND EARTH, however greatly the affairs and cares of this world do trouble, molest, and avert us from rendering unto thee that honour and obedience due unto thee, yet we beseech thee that, forgetting all other things, we may have no other aim but to praise and glorify thee all the days of our life, for the great benefits which we continually receive at thy hands, through Jesus Christ our Lord. Amen.

Psalm 135

O LORD GOD, who by thy dear Son Jesus Christ hast made us kings and priests to offer unto thee spiritual sacrifices, grant unto us that we, renouncing all idolatry, superstition, and all ungodliness, may give over ourselves to thy service; and that in all times of tribulation we may call upon thee with our whole heart, that we may feel thy fatherly bounty and mercy which thou art wont to use toward all them whom thou hast regenerated through the self-same Jesus Christ. AMEN.

Psalm 136

GRACIOUS FATHER, replenished with all glory and magnificence, grant unto us of thy merciful grace that we may so apply ourselves to the consideration of thy marvel-lous works and mighty providence, whereby thou disposest and settest all things in good and due order, that thereby we may take occasion to celebrate thy praises without ceasing; and specially inasmuch as thou hast renewed us by thy Holy Spirit, that thereby we may finally enjoy life eternal which thy Son, Christ Jesus, has got for us with his blood. AMEN.

Psalm 137

MERCIFUL LORD, the comforter and deliverer of poor captives, thou seest the great extremities whereinto thy poor church is brought and how she is on all hands exposed to the slavery and mockery of thine enemies and ours, scoffing and

attainting [accusing] both us and thy praises.
O God, turn back thy wrath upon them, and
hear us who mourn and sigh for our deliverance; so that, the tyrants our persecutors
being overthrown, we may freely sing thy
praises and lauds in thy house, in the name
of Jesus Christ our Lord. AMEN.

Psalm 138

MIGHTY LORD, full of peace and goodness, who hast ever borne such favour
unto thy church that even strange nations
have been compelled to acknowledge and
praise thy marvellous bounty whereby thou
dost exalt the disdained and contemptible,
and dost cast down the proud and haughty,
make, Lord, all people to submit under

thy mighty hand; and preserve us from all calamities; that all the world may know thou wilt not leave the work imperfect which thou hast begun in us, through Jesus Christ, thy Son. AMEN.

Psalm 139

O LOVING FATHER, unto whom both we and all inward secrets of our hearts are known, grant unto us that we may so walk before thee in uprightness of conscience that we keep no company with mockers and contemners of thy holy Word. But may we be so circumcised in heart and mind that, renouncing all worldly friendship, we may never stray from the right way which thou hast shown forth to us in the Evangel of Jesus Christ, our only Saviour. AMEN.

Psalm 140

Deliver me, O LORD, from the wicked and ungodly men, who in their hearts devise mischief and delight in strife and contention, whose tongues are sharp as serpents', yea, the venom of adders lurks under their lips. Lord, let us us not fall into their gins [traps], neither suffer them to handle us according to their desires. Thou art our God; hear the voice of our complaints; take the defence of our cause in thy hand, that we may with all our hearts render thee hearty praises and thanks, through Jesus Christ our Lord. AMEN.

Psalm 141

To thee, O LORD, we cry; hear us, we beseech thee. Let our prayer be as a sweet savour before thee, and the lifting up of our hands as an evening sacrifice. Set a watch before our mouth and keep the door of our lips that they speak no proud thing, as the wicked do; but that they may call upon thee in all uprightness and simplicity. Finally, let us cast our eyes on thee in only trust, and in thee alone repose ourselves. Suffer us not to perish, but deliver us from the snares which the wicked have prepared for us, and that through Jesus Christ our Saviour. Amen.

Psalm 142

Unto thee, Lord, the protector and defender of all them that trust in thy clemency, we cry and put forth our sighs; unto thee we open and lay bare the troubles of our hearts. Thou knowest our ways and distresses, and how on all parts we are circled and compassed with cruel and ungodly enemies. Deliver us, dear Father, from those troubles and dangers wherein we are, and declare the care thou hast for us who love and honour thee; that we may in the midst of thy holy congregation render thee perpetual thanks, and that through Jesus Christ, thy dear Son, our only Saviour. AMEN.

Psalm 143

O GOD, hear our prayers and receive our complaints; refuse us not for thy righteousness' sake. Enter not into judgment with us thy servants, for we know, if thou dealest strictly, no man, not even the most holy, may stand in judgment before thee. Teach us therefore, O Father, to do thy will, and let thy Holy Spirit lead us in all our ways, that they may be agreeable to thy ordinances, and that through Jesus Christ thy Son. AMEN.

Psalm 144

POWERFUL GOD OF ARMIES, who knowest our weakness and infirmities to be so great that by ourselves we are not able to stand up for a moment before our adversaries, did thy mighty power not uphold us, bow down thyself out of the heavens, and stretch forth thy strong hand, that those who seek our ruin may see thou art our protector and defender. Give us such prosperous success that all the world may see that those are not miserable who depend on thee, and claim thee to be their God, through Jesus Christ our Saviour. AMEN.

Psalm 145

Thy mercies, LORD, are above all thy works; faithful art thou in all thy promises, and just in all thy doings. Be a merciful Father unto us for Christ Jesus thy Son's sake. Govern our ways for we are weak; strengthen us for we are frail; refresh us for we are famished; and plentifully bestow thy good gifts upon us. Defend us from the snares of Satan, our old enemy, that he tempt us not out of the right way, but that we be evermore ready to praise and glorify thy holy name, through Jesus Christ. AMEN.

Psalm 146

O GOOD GOD, suffer not that in any wise we set thee aside to put our trust or confidence in princes or in the children of men; but let us continually have all our trust and confidence fixed upon thee, for unto such as do so thou art a sure rock and refuge. Lead, Lord, them that walk in darkness; deliver the oppressed; enlarge thy kingdom, which all thy chosen children who are redeemed by the blood of thy Son most earnestly thirst for; and that for the same Jesus Christ's sake. AMEN.

Psalm 147

O LORD, marvellous are thy might and strength, whereby thou castest down the proud and fearful tyrant and liftest up the humble and meek ones. We beseech thee of thy great mercy to restore and rebuild thy church, which was founded by thee only. Gather together thy scattered sheep; and as thou feedest all creatures with temporal food and pasturage, make us to have an inward feeling of the effect of thy holy Word, that we, following thy will declared therein, may in the end enjoy the heritage prepared for us in Christ Jesus. AMEN.

Psalm 148

Great and marvellous is thy majesty, O MIGHTY GOD, Maker and Conserver of all things and mightily doth it shine in all thy creatures, both in heaven and earth and in the sea. Grant that, as these all acknowledge thee, so we may also make acknowledgment of the same, that with one accord and uniform consent we may with thy holy angels praise the magnificence of thy glorious name; so that all may rejoice in the health and exalting of thy people, whom thou hast relieved from death through the blood of Jesus Christ. AMEN.

Psalm 149

Instruct our mouths, O GOOD LORD, with a new song, that, our hearts being renewed, we may sing in the company of thy saints, and rejoice in thee our Creator and Redeemer. Let us possess such peace of conscience as may strongly work for thee. And, being girded with the two-edged sword of thy Word and Holy Spirit, may we strive against all things that oppose themselves to the glory of thy most holy name, and that through Jesus Christ, thy dear Son, our only Lord and Redeemer. AMEN.

Psalm 150

Most worthy art thou, O GOOD AND GRACIOUS GOD, of all praises, even for thine own sake, surpassing all things in holiness. By thee alone are we made holy and sanctified. We praise thee for our glorious redemption, purchased for us in thy dearly beloved Son, Christ Jesus, as our duty continually bids us. Give us thy Holy Spirit to govern us. And grant that all things which breathe with life may praise thee as the true life of all creatures, through the same Jesus Christ our Lord, who reigneth with thee and the Holy Ghost, one God, for ever and ever. AMEN.

Because you are but a young man, beware of temptations and snares; and above all, be careful to keep yourself in the use of means; resort to good company; and howbeit you be nicknamed a Puritan, and mocked, yet care not for that, but rejoice and be glad, that they who are scorned and scoffed by this godless and vain world, and nicknamed Puritans, would admit you to their society; for I must tell you, when I am at this point as you see me, I get no comfort to my soul by any second means under heaven but from those who are nicknamed Puritans. They are the men that can give a word of comfort to a wearied soul in due season, and that I have found by experience ...

THE LAST AND HEAVENLY SPEECHES, AND
GLORIOUS DEPARTURE, OF JOHN, VISCOUNT KENMURE

OTHER
POCKET PURITANS

Am I a Christian? James Fraser
Anger Management Richard Baxter
Binge Drinking John Flavel
A Guide to Christian Living John Calvin (gift ed.)
Heaven, a World of Love Jonathan Edwards
Impure Lust John Flavel
Living Faith Samuel Ward
The Loveliness of Christ Samuel Rutherford (gift ed.)
Pastoral Ministry Richard Baxter
Repent and Believe! Thomas Brooks
Sampler from A Way to Pray Matthew Henry
The Shorter Catechism with Scripture Proofs
Sinful Speech John Flavel
Truth For All Time John Calvin (gift ed.)
United We Stand Thomas Brooks
When Christians Suffer Thomas Case

For more details of all Banner publications,
including the Puritan Paperback series and
our reprints of the works of the Puritans,
please visit our website:

www.banneroftruth.co.uk

THE BANNER OF TRUTH TRUST

3 Murrayfield Road,
Edinburgh EH12 6EL
UK

P O Box 621, Carlisle,
PA 17013,
USA

www.banneroftruth.co.uk